CHRISTMAS CRAFTS

WITHDRAWN

written by
Judy Ann Sadler

illustrated by Marilyn Mets

KIDS CAN PRESS LTD.
Toronto

To Jeff, for making every day seem like Christmas Day

Special thanks to Joanne de Kort, Laila Hillo,
Vince Madamba and Karen Shadd-Evelyn for sharing with
me their knowledge of Christmas in other countries —JAS

Canadian Cataloguing in Publication Data

Sadler, Judy Ann, 1959-
Christmas crafts

(Kids can easy crafts)
ISBN 1-55074-189-6

1. Christmas decorations — Juvenile literature.
2. Handicraft — Juvenile literature. I. Mets, Marilyn.
II. Title. III. Series.

TT900.C4S3 1994   j745.594'12   C94-930783-1

Published in Canada by
Kids Can Press Ltd.
29 Birch Avenue
Toronto, ON M4V 1E2

Edited by Laurie Wark
Designed by N.R. Jackson
Printed in Hong Kong

KCP/CM 94 0 9 8 7 6 5

CONTENTS

GETTING STARTED

What are the traditional things you do every year at Christmas time? Do you sing your favourite carols, visit special people or eat once-a-year treats? There are so many interesting ways to celebrate this holiday. People in some parts of the world cosy up to a Yule-log, while others spend the day picnicking on the beach. Some people parade noisily to church, while others gather with their families for a candlelit meal. These traditions make Christmas a magical time of year.

Although people celebrate Christmas in different ways, many people like to make things at Christmas time. In this book you will find out how to make many of the ornaments that decorate homes around the world. You can make a German Advent calendar to count down the number of days until Christmas. Create a Mexican piñata for a party. Surprise a friend with a Danish woven basket filled with treats. Make garlands, wreaths and a beautiful nativity scene that will last for years. Store your finished projects in labelled shoeboxes, plastic containers or large envelopes so they are ready for the next holiday season.

Dig out your old Christmas cards, wrapping paper, pipe cleaners and felt, and create these crafts from around the world. Merry Christmas craftmaking!

Materials

felt Felt is an easy material to use. It does not ravel, it can be ironed with a damp cloth and it comes in many colours. Use real felt, not acrylic, for the projects in this book because acrylic felt does not glue together very well.

string Many of the ornaments in this book are hung from yarn, string or ribbon. You can use whatever you have around home or buy the fancy kind that is available at Christmas time.

scissors You will need scissors sharp enough to cut felt and strong enough to cut pipe cleaners.

glue Use good-quality, clear-drying, non-toxic white glue.

other stuff You will find most of the other things you need around home or at your local craft supply store.

ENGLISH POMANDER

This traditional, spicy-smelling orange pomander reminds people of the warm, sunny days they will enjoy after the dark days of winter are over. **Season's Greetings!**

THINGS YOU NEED:

orange (at room temperature)
clear tape (or narrow masking tape)
small nail or round toothpick
cloves
scissors
satin ribbon 6 to 10 mm
   ($^1/_4$ to $^1/_2$ inch) wide
ruler

1 Starting at the top, circle the orange with two lines of tape so that it looks as if it has been divided into quarters.

2 Use the nail to poke a hole near the top of the orange and beside the piece of tape. Gently push in a clove. Keep poking holes and pushing in cloves until you have cloves along both sides of both lines of tape.

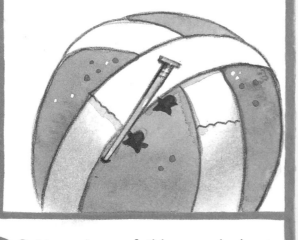

3 Carefully remove the tape.

4 Cut two pieces of ribbon, each about 70 cm (28 inches) long.

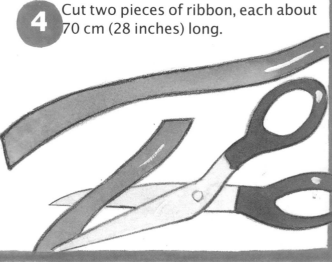

5 Bring one ribbon around the orange in the space where the tape was and tie it in a single loop at the top. Let the ends hang down.

6 Bring the second ribbon around the orange along the other tape line. Tie it into a bow on top of the first ribbon.

7 Bring together the ends from the first ribbon and knot them so that you now have a loop to hang up your pomander. The orange will shrink over the next few weeks, but by undoing the bow and re-tying it, you will make the ribbons snug again.

Fun ideas to try

Pattern the cloves into swirls or diamonds or completely cover the orange with cloves. Gently tie a ribbon around the pomander to hang it up, or put it into a drawer.

Use sequins and small beads on pins to decorate the pomander.

NORWEGIAN REINDEER

In some parts of the world, people believe that gifts are carried by a goat or a horse. People who live in cold places, like Norway, say that reindeer are the best helpers because they have large hooves to help them pull a sled full of gifts through heavy snow. **Gledelig Jul!**

THINGS YOU NEED:

scissors
thread
ruler
glue
3 flat craft clothespegs,
  all the same size
felt scraps
roly eyes, beads, mini pompoms
  or markers

1 Cut a piece of thread 30 cm (12 inches) long. Fold it in half and make a small knot in it.

2 Put glue on the top half of one clothespeg. Place the knot of thread in the glue and hold the second peg against it as the glue begins to dry.

3 Put glue on the top half of the second peg. Place the third peg on the glue upside down, so that it looks like a reindeer head and antlers.

4 Finish your reindeer by giving it small felt ears and a short felt tail. Use roly eyes, beads, pompoms, felt or markers to make the face. If you want, you can tie a small bell or ribbon around your reindeer's neck.

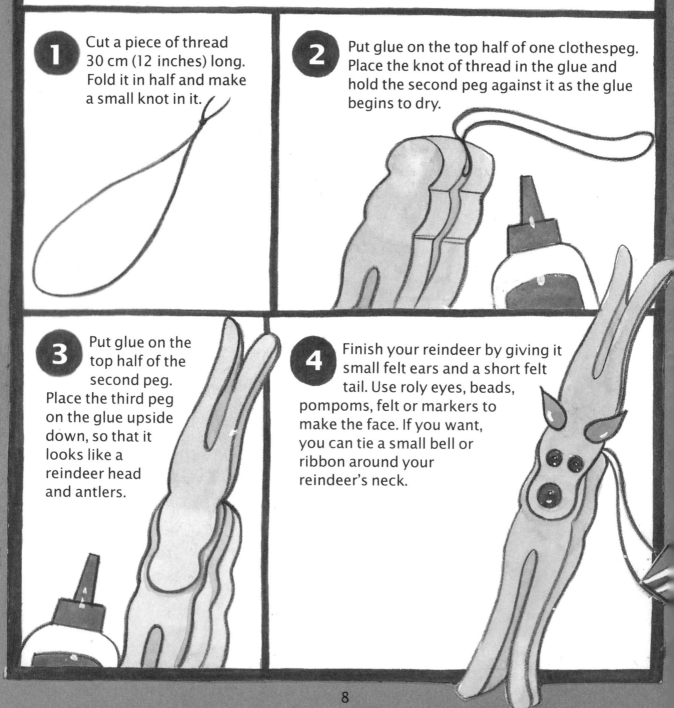

FINNISH FLAG GARLANDS

In Finland, some people decorate their Christmas trees with garlands of mini-flags from around the world. **Hauskaa Joulua!**

THINGS YOU NEED:

pencil
ruler
thin cardboard
scissors
plain paper
pictures of flags from around the world
markers, crayons or pencil crayons
yarn or heavy string
glue

1 Draw a rectangle 4 cm x 13 cm (1½ inches x 5 inches) on the cardboard. Cut it out.

2 Use this pattern to trace many rectangles onto plain paper. Draw a line down the middle of each rectangle.

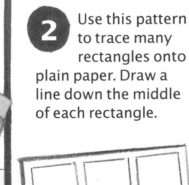

3 Using the pictures of flags as guides, draw and colour in flags on the right half of each rectangle. Write each flag's country on the left side.

FINLAND

4 Cut out the flags and fold them in half over the string. Glue them onto the string, leaving about 15 cm (6 inches) between each flag.

IRISH CANDLES

Candles are an important part of Christmas celebrations everywhere. In Ireland, families put candles in the windows on Christmas Eve to welcome Mary and Joseph and to light the way to church for passers-by. **Nollaig Shona Dhuit!**

THINGS YOU NEED:

sheet of beeswax, any colour
waxed paper
long ruler or straight edge
scissors
candlewick

1 Place the beeswax on a sheet of waxed paper. Lay the ruler on the beeswax diagonally, from corner to corner. Use scissors to mark a light line along this straight edge.

2 Cut the wax along the line. You will now have two long triangles. Set one aside to make another candle later.

3 Cut a piece of candlewick about 5 cm (2 inches) longer than the shortest side of your triangle. Place the wick along the short edge of the triangle so that some of it hangs over at both ends.

4 To start the candle, roll and press the edge of the wax into the wick. It helps if your hands are warm. If the wax cracks a little, press it firmly over the wick and it will stick together.

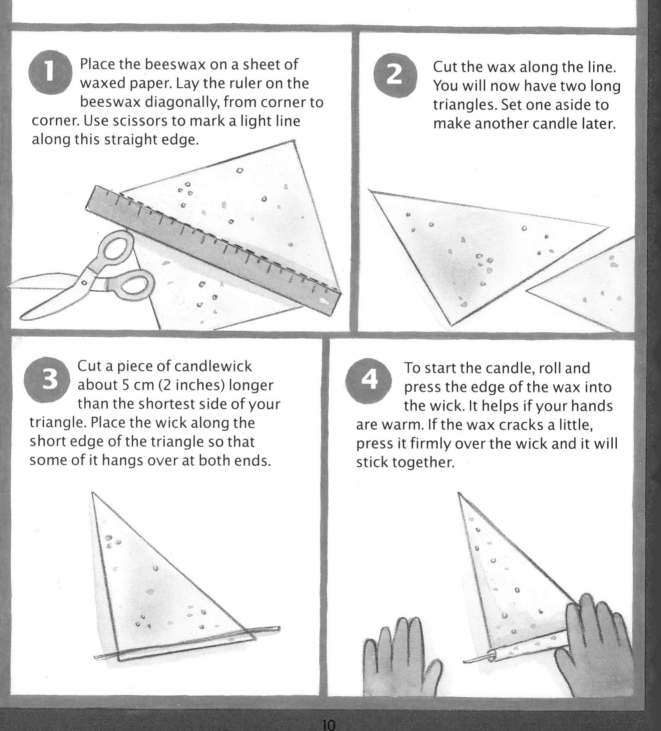

5 Tightly roll the wax, keeping the straight edge even.

6 As you finish the candle, roll it firmly across the waxed paper to make the end stick in place. If the bottom is uneven, gently push it down against the waxed-paper surface to make it as flat as you can.

7 Cut off the wick at the bottom and trim it to 1 cm (1/2 inch) on top. If you are not going to burn the candle now, store it in a sheet of waxed paper.

8 Place the candle in a holder that can fit different-sized candles. Be sure to ask an adult to light it for you, and make sure you blow it out when you leave the room.

Fun ideas to try

Cut the sheet of beeswax in half lengthwise first and then cut it diagonally, to make shorter candles. Or cut straight strips and simply roll them up with a piece of wick inside. These types of candles may not fit into a regular holder, so firmly set them on a non-flammable surface to burn them.

Try rolling two colours of wax together for a whole new look.

Cut out little wax holly leaves, hearts, stars or other shapes, and press them onto your candle to decorate it.

CHINESE LANTERNS

When Chinese artists painted the Nativity, they showed angels holding decorated lanterns as they gazed upon the Holy Family. **Sheng Dan Kuai Le!**

THINGS YOU NEED:

used greeting cards
scissors
ruler
glue

1 Cut off the front of the card. Fold it in half lengthwise so that the picture is showing.

2 Hold the card with the open end up. Make cuts 1 cm (½ inch) apart along the folded edge. The cuts should end 1 cm (½ inch) from the top edge.

3 Open the card and glue the sides together. Hold it for a moment while the glue dries.

4 For the handle, cut a strip from the back of the card or from another card front. The strip should be about 15 cm (6 inches) long. Glue the ends across from each other on the inside of the top of the lantern. Make more lanterns.

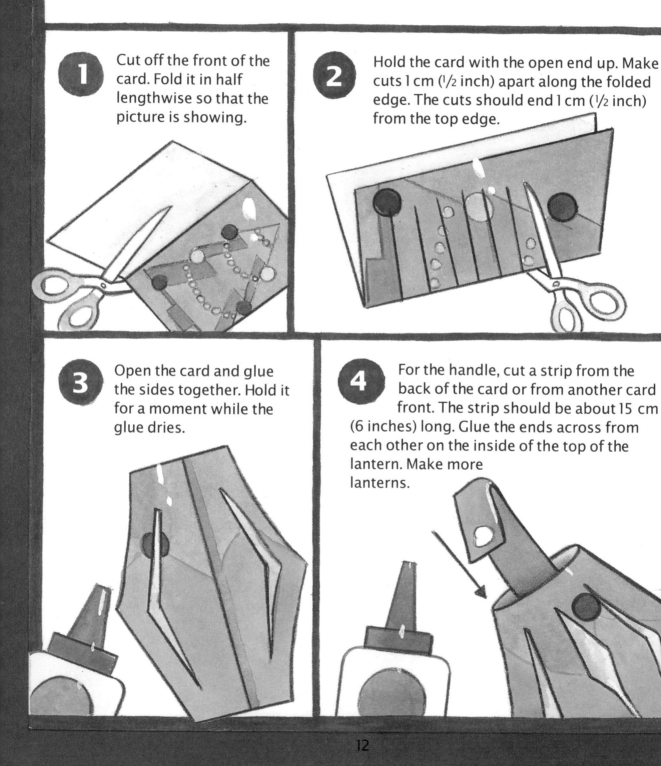

5 Cut strips of card fronts and backs about 1 cm (½ inch) wide and 10 to 15 cm (4 to 6 inches) long. Glue one strip into a circle. Put another strip through the circle and glue that strip into a circle. Keep going until you have a chain long enough to hang in a doorway or across a room.

6 Attach the handles of the lanterns to the chain. Space them evenly and hang up your Chinese-lantern garland.

Fun ideas to try

Put some crumpled yellow tissue paper in the lantern to make it look like candlelight.

Try making lanterns with construction paper, wrapping paper or white paper that you've decorated.

Decorate the lanterns by wrapping tinsel pipe cleaners around the top and bottom or by gluing on sparkles or strips of foil.

DANISH WOVEN BASKETS

In Denmark, families make these small heart-shaped baskets, fill them with goodies and hang them from their Christmas trees.
Glaedelig Jul!

THINGS YOU NEED:

scissors
ruler
2 pieces of different-coloured, shiny paper (traditionally they are red and white)
glue

1 Cut a rectangle 6 cm x 20 cm (2¼ inches x 8 inches) out of each piece of paper.

2 Fold the rectangles in half. Hold each one so that the open edges are at the top. Round off the top corners.

3 Cut two slits up from the folded edge, making them 2 cm (¾ inch) apart and 7 cm (2¾ inches) long.

4 Start weaving one part into the other as shown. Tuck 1 between the layers of C, tuck B between the layers of 1, and 1 between the layers of A. Slide the woven part up a little and now tuck C between 2, 2 between B, and A between 2. Finally, tuck 3 inside C, B inside 3, and 3 inside A. You should be able to see the pattern on the inside as well as on the front and back when you open your basket.

5 Glue a handle between the two woven layers on each side of the heart.

6 Fill your basket with nuts, candies or other treats, and hang it on your tree or give it as a gift.

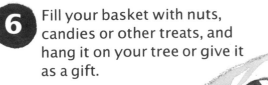

Fun ideas to try

 Make baskets using felt. Cut tiny slits in the top so that you can tie on ribbon handles.

Cut the rectangles out of wrapping paper that is white on the back. Fold one rectangle so that the pattern is showing and the other so that the white is showing.

FRENCH STAINED-GLASS STAR

The first large stained-glass windows were made for French Gothic-style churches over eight hundred years ago. Some of the most beautiful stained-glass windows show Mary, Joseph and baby Jesus on the first Christmas. **Joyeux Noël!**

THINGS YOU NEED:

construction paper
pencil
scissors
many colours of tissue
   paper
waxed paper
ruler
iron, ironing board and
   two cloth rags
glue

1 Fold a piece of construction paper in half widthwise. Draw half of a large star along the folded edge as shown. (You may want to experiment on scrap paper first, but the star does not need to be perfect.)

2 Leave the paper folded and cut out the half star. Cut out the inside of the star so that when you open it, you have a star frame.

3 Cut pieces of tissue paper into many small shapes.

4 Tear off two sheets of waxed paper, each 30 cm (12 inches) long. Put a smooth cloth on the ironing board and place one sheet of waxed paper on the cloth.

5 Place the tissue-paper shapes all over the waxed paper. Try not to leave bare spaces but don't overlap them too much.

6 Gently place the other sheet of waxed paper on top of the shapes. Ask an adult to cover it with another cloth and press with a hot iron. Turn it over and iron the other side, too. Make sure that all the tissue pieces have melted wax either on the front or on the back. If they do not, they may need more ironing.

7 Run a line of glue around your star frame. Glue it onto the pressed tissue paper and hold it down firmly. Let the glue dry for a few minutes.

8 Cut around the star shape. If the two sheets of waxed paper have come apart along the newly cut edges, glue them together. Hang your stained-glass star in a window.

Fun ideas to try

 Try making a heart or a peaked church-window shape.

 Make mini-shapes from the pressed tissue paper that you cut off, and hang them on the tree.

JAPANESE ORIGAMI ORNAMENTS

Christmas is the perfect time to decorate your home with folded paper ornaments made using the ancient Japanese art of origami. **Meri Kurisumasu!**

THINGS YOU NEED:

ruler
pencil
scissors
thin cardboard
wrapping paper, construction paper or
   any colourful scrap paper

1 Measure and cut out a 13 cm x 13 cm (5 inch x 5 inch) square of cardboard. Use it as a guide to draw and cut out squares of paper.

2 Fold a square in half so that, if it has a patterned side, that side is on the inside and not showing. Open the square and fold it the other way, again with the pattern not showing.

3 Open the square and fold it in half diagonally, this time with the patterned side on the outside. Open it and fold it across the other two corners.

4 Open the square again and hold it with the patterned side up. Push in the sides until the paper forms a triangle shape. Smooth the folds. Make many more origami triangles and try the ideas on the next page.

GARLAND Thread yarn into a needle and knot one end. Bring the needle up from underneath the triangle and poke it through the centre. Pull the yarn through until the knot stops it from going any farther. Tie a knot in the yarn about 8 cm (3 inches) above the triangle, and thread on another triangle. Keep adding knots and triangles. Hang the string on the tree, in an archway, a window, or any other place that needs decorating. Try this idea with mini-triangles, too.

GREETING CARD Fold a sheet of construction paper to make a card. Cut out three different-sized squares of paper and fold them into triangles. Glue the smallest one near the top of the card. Glue the middle-sized triangle below it and the largest one on the bottom. Cut out a little star and glue it at the top of your Christmas tree.

ORNAMENT Glue together two squares of paper, wrong sides together, and then fold this square into a triangle. Stretch it out a little so that it looks like a four-pointed star. Thread a string through one of the points and hang up the star.

VICTORIAN DECORATIONS

In the 1800s, when it became popular to decorate a Christmas tree, people made decorations from things they found around home.

Paper-Cone Decorations

THINGS YOU NEED:

cup about 7 cm (2 3/4 inches) across
pencil
construction or wrapping paper or used
    Christmas cards
scissors
glue
string or ribbon

1 Use the cup to trace about ten circles onto the paper, and cut out the circles. Fold each circle in half, unfold it and cut it along the fold line.

2 Glue each half circle into a cone. If you are using wrapping paper or cards, glue the cone so that the pattern is on the inside. If your paper is stiff, you will need to hold the cone for a moment while the glue dries.

3 Glue two cones together on the side so that their points are touching. Put a line of glue on each cone and add a third cone. Keep adding cones, points together in the centre, until you have a globe.

4 Gently roll and pat the ornament in your hands to make sure that all the cones are stuck together. Tie a knot in the string. Squirt glue into one of the spaces between the cones. Push the knotted end of the string into the glue and let it dry before you hang the globe up.

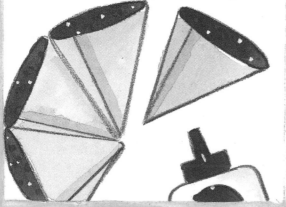

GARLANDS Cut strips of paper 1 to 2 cm ($\frac{1}{2}$ to $\frac{3}{4}$ inch) wide and 15 to 20 cm (6 to 8 inches) long. Glue one strip into a circle and loop the next one through it, and so on. Try this with old greeting cards, ribbon (you may need to use tape instead of glue), scraps of wrapping paper or fabric. Also, try gluing sparkles onto a sheet of construction paper and then cutting it into strips to make sparkling garland. You can also make garlands by stringing cut-up straws, paper hearts and stars, beads and pasta.

SNOWFLAKES Use cups, bowls and plastic containers to trace different-sized circles onto paper. Cut them out. Fold each one in half and then in thirds. Cut out pieces along the sides and at the top and bottom. Open them and run a string through one of the holes. Hang the snowflakes on the Christmas tree, in doorways, from garlands or in windows.

POPCORN STRINGS

Make lots of popcorn without butter and salt. Thread a long, strong piece of thread into a needle and poke it through a piece of popcorn. Be careful not to prick your fingers. Thread on about five pieces of popcorn and then thread on a cranberry or a red bead. Keep threading until you have enough to go around the tree (you can tie short popcorn strings together). If you use beads instead of cranberries, you can store your popcorn string in a box and use it next year.

CORNUCOPIAS Use a bowl or plate to trace circles onto paper. Fold and cut the circles in half. Decorate them with crayons, markers, sparkles, fabric, wrapping paper or paper doilies. Glue or staple them into cones and add a handle. Fill the cones with candies or a small gift, and hang them on the tree.

ANCIENT ROMAN WREATH

In ancient Rome, people made evergreen wreaths to symbolize the continual cycle of the seasons and life. The wreaths reminded them that there was life even in the cold, dark days of winter and that spring would return. Now we make wreaths out of all kinds of things to add colour and beauty to our homes, especially at Christmas.

THINGS YOU NEED:

wire clothes hanger
scissors or pinking
  shears
Christmas fabric
ruler
masking tape

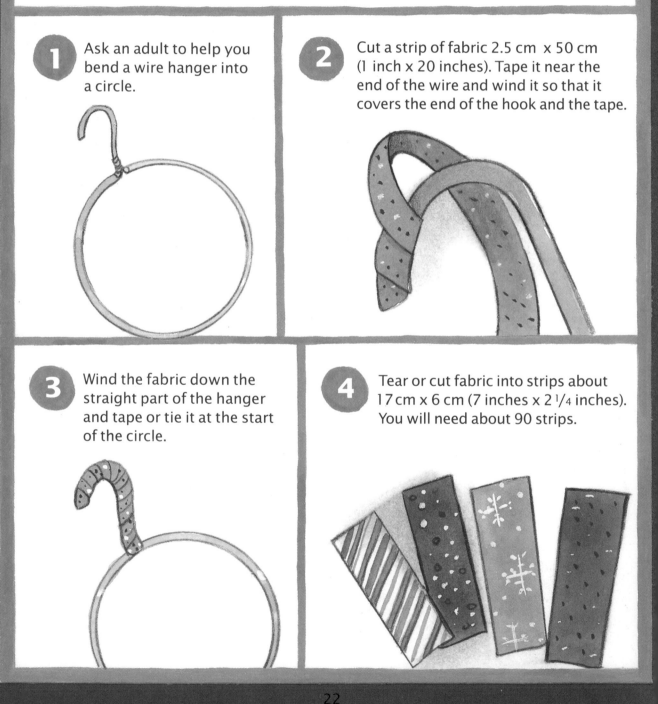

1 Ask an adult to help you bend a wire hanger into a circle.

2 Cut a strip of fabric 2.5 cm x 50 cm (1 inch x 20 inches). Tape it near the end of the wire and wind it so that it covers the end of the hook and the tape.

3 Wind the fabric down the straight part of the hanger and tape or tie it at the start of the circle.

4 Tear or cut fabric into strips about 17 cm x 6 cm (7 inches x 2 1/4 inches). You will need about 90 strips.

22

5 Tie the strips onto the circle. Tightly tie them once — they don't need to be knotted.

6 Slide the fabric strips around the wire until they are packed on tightly. Fluff them and trim off any loose threads. Hang up your new wreath.

Fun ideas to try

 Use a variety of materials, such as streamers, wide ribbon, felt and colourful plastic bags, to make a wreath.

Decorate your wreath with ribbon or fabric bows, tree decorations or silk flowers.

ITALIAN NATIVITY SCENE

*Eight hundred years ago, Saint Francis of Assisi is said to have gathered together real people and animals to re-create the first Christmas. Today, many families display handmade nativity figures in their homes at Christmas. **Buon Natale!***

THINGS YOU NEED:

scissors
felt
ruler
long pipe cleaners, 30 cm (12 inches) long
short pipe cleaners, 15 cm (6 inches) long
glue
wooden beads (20-mm size)
acrylic paints, markers or bits of paper

1 Cut out a rectangle of felt 12 cm x 22 cm (4½ inches x 8½ inches). Fold it in half lengthwise, then widthwise to find the centre. Make a small cut at this centre point.

2 Bend a long pipe cleaner in half. Wrap a short pipe cleaner once around the long one 2 cm (¾ inch) down from the folded end. These are your figure's arms, neck and body.

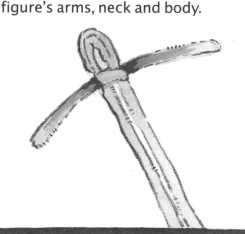

3 Slip the neck through the hole in the felt rectangle. Bend the pipe cleaner hands around the edge of the felt to hold the robe in place.

4 Spread glue on the neck and put on the wooden-bead head.

5 Bend the arms at the elbows and move them forward. This should bring the felt robe together in the front. Overlap and glue it. Trim off the pipe cleaners (and the felt robe if you need to) so that your figure can stand up. If you want your figure to kneel, bend it at the knees.

6 Use the ideas below to make Mary, Joseph, the kings, a shepherd or an angel. Use acrylic paint, markers or bits of paper to make the faces.

MARY Give Mary yarn hair. Cut a strip of felt for her to wear over her head. You can bend her arms to hold baby Jesus.

SHEPHERD Give him a pipe-cleaner staff so that he can herd his sheep.

ANGEL Dress the angel in white. Cut out a large white heart and glue it on her back to make wings. Make a pipe-cleaner halo and poke it down the hole in the bead head.

JOSEPH Use a marker, paint or yarn to give Joseph hair and a beard.

KINGS Dress them in purple, blue and red robes. Cut out crowns from shiny greeting cards and glue them on. You can give the kings gifts to bring to baby Jesus, too.

BABY JESUS Poke a 2.5-cm (1-inch) piece of pipe cleaner into a small wooden bead. Cut a 1 cm x 8 cm ($1/2$ inch x 3 inch) strip of felt to glue around the baby's head and tuck under his chin. Twist the felt around the pipe cleaner to hold it in place. Cut another piece of felt to wrap and glue around the baby like a blanket.

OTHER NATIVITY FIGURES

Many nativity scenes include the animals, the stable and manger and the star shining overhead.

Sheep

THINGS YOU NEED:

scissors
white, beige or black yarn
ruler
dark pipe cleaners

1 Cut five lengths of yarn, each 75 cm (30 inches) long. Untwist the strands of yarn so that you now have kinky strands.

2 Cut a 15-cm (6-inch) piece of pipe cleaner and bend both ends towards the centre. Now bend one end down to make the nose. Raise the neck up and push the tail down.

3 Cut a 4-cm (1¹/₂-inch) piece of pipe cleaner and wrap it around the head to make ears. Cut two 8-cm (3-inch) pieces and wrap them around the body to make four legs.

4 Loosely wrap the kinky yarn around the sheep's frame. Leave the ears, nose, legs and tail unwrapped. You don't need to glue the yarn ends because they won't show. Add the sheep to your nativity scene or sit it in the Christmas tree.

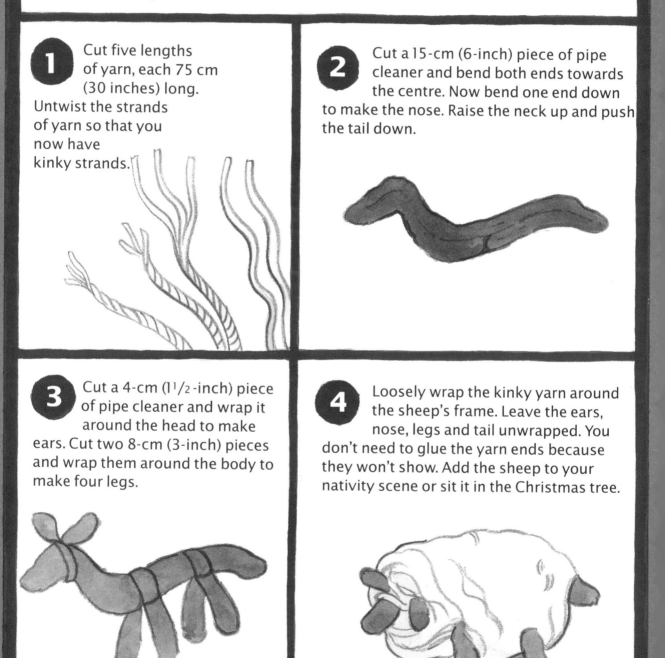

STABLE Cut two simple house shapes out of cardboard. Cut one in half and lay it over the full house shape as shown. To make hinges, cut four short pieces of ribbon. Tape them, two on each side, to the half houses. Now flip the house shapes over and tape the other end of the ribbon onto the back. Open the half houses and set up the stable. If it doesn't stand, it may need to be trimmed along the bottom. Place your nativity figures in and around the stable.

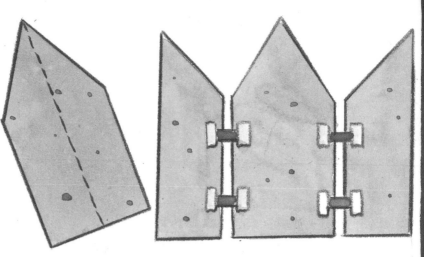

MANGER Cut a bathroom-tissue roll in half lengthwise and cut off a piece about 6 cm (2 1/4 inches) long. Line it with some felt. Cut up yellow yarn to look like straw. Place baby Jesus in the manger.

STAR Bend the first 2.5 cm (1 inch) of a long tinsel (or regular) pipe cleaner. Now bend the rest of it into a zigzag pattern using the bent end as a guide. Shape the pipe cleaner into a five-pointed star. Twist the ends around each other and trim off any extra. Hang the star from the top of the stable.

GERMAN ADVENT CALENDAR

Children in Germany were the first to count down the number of days until Christmas with an Advent calendar. Now this tradition has spread around the world.
Fröhliche Weihnachten!

THINGS YOU NEED:

scissors
long ruler or measuring tape
red and green felt
glue
permanent marker or fabric paint in a squirt bottle
large piece of paper or sheet of newspaper
pencil
dried sliver of soap or chalk
scraps of felt
thin dowel or any straight stick about 55 cm
   (22 inches) long
string or yarn

1 Cut a large rectangle 48 cm x 60 cm (19 inches x 24 inches) out of the red felt. Place the rectangle on your work table, the long way up.

2 To make pockets, cut three strips of green felt, each 48 cm x 4 cm (19 inches x 1½ inches). Run a line of glue along the bottom only of each strip and glue them in rows at the bottom of the red felt. Glue down the ends of each strip.

3 To divide each strip into eight pockets, dab a bit of glue in seven evenly spaced places on the underside of each strip and press the glue spots down. Number the pockets from 1 to 24 with a permanent marker or fabric paint.

4 Turn over the red felt and run a line of glue along the top. Fold the felt down about 4 cm (1½ inches) and pat it until the glue starts to dry. Turn the felt over again.

5 Fold the large sheet of paper in half. Draw a half Christmas tree along the fold and cut it out. Open it. The tree should be about 35 cm (14 inches) tall and 45 cm (18 inches) wide at the widest branches.

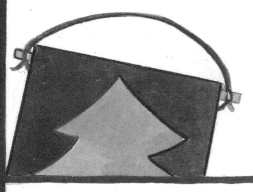

6 Use the chalk or soap to trace your tree pattern onto the green felt. Cut the tree out. Also cut out a small brown trunk. Glue the tree and trunk to the red felt.

7 Push the stick through the pocket along the top. Cut a piece of string, ribbon or yarn 75 cm (30 inches) long. Tie the string to each end of the stick so that you can hang up your calendar.

8 Cut out 24 felt Christmas symbols, such as holly, candy canes, gingerbread, gift boxes, snowflakes, bells, candles and stars. Make sure they are small enough to fit into the pockets. Starting on December 1st, take out a decoration each day and pat it gently onto the tree. When all the pockets are empty, Christmas has arrived!

MEXICAN PIÑATA

In Mexico, the nine days before Christmas are called Posadas. On these evenings, people dress up and act out Mary and Joseph looking for a place to stay. Afterwards they have a celebration with food, music and piñatas. **Feliz Navidad!**

THINGS YOU NEED:

newspaper
ruler
1 medium-sized round or oval balloon
2 mixing bowls, 1 small and 1 medium
measuring cups and spoons
flour
salt
water
scissors
string or yarn
tissue paper
pencil with an eraser
glue

1 Spread newspaper on your work table. Tear other sheets of newspaper into strips about 4 cm x 20 cm (1 1/2 inches x 8 inches).

2 Blow up the balloon and knot it. Sit it on the small mixing bowl.

3 To make papier-mâché paste, mix together 175 mL (3/4 cups) of flour, 30 mL (2 tablespoons) of salt and 350 mL (1 1/2 cups) of water in the other bowl. Use your fingers to get out the lumps.

4 Dip a newspaper strip into the paste. As you take the strip out, run it between your fingers to get off the extra paste. Smooth the strip onto the balloon.

5 Criss-cross strips of newspaper everywhere on the balloon except for an area about 8 cm (3 inches) around the knot. Turn the balloon on the bowl as you work.

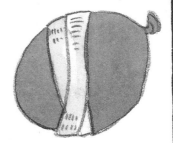

6 If your papier-mâché balloon gets too wet, smooth on some dry strips. You should have four or five layers of newspaper on the balloon.

7 Leave the piñata on the bowl and turn it every few hours, or place it on a cooling rack to dry. Depending on how wet your piñata is, it will take from 16 to 48 hours to dry.

8 When you are sure the piñata is dry (check by feeling around the open edges on top), pop the balloon and take it out.

9 Use scissors to carefully poke three evenly spaced holes 2.5 cm (1 inch) down from the top. Cut three pieces of yarn or string, each 1 m (3 feet) long. Pull one piece halfway through each hole and knot all six ends together. Now turn the page to find out how to decorate your piñata.

10 Cut many sheets of different-coloured tissue paper into 8 cm x 8 cm (3 inch x 3 inch) squares. Poke the eraser end of your pencil into the centre of a square of tissue paper, scrunch the tissue around the pencil and dip it into glue.

11 Press the tissue onto the piñata. Cover the outside of your piñata with these tissue-paper tufts starting at the bottom and working your way up. When you are finished, glue a few long strips of tissue paper to the bottom of the piñata for decoration.

12 Put in nuts, wrapped candies, coins, jokes and other surprises. Be careful not to make your piñata too heavy. Hang it from the ceiling or tie it on a stick and have someone hold it up high. Now you are ready for a piñata party.

Everyone should stand in a circle around the piñata. One player at a time is blindfolded, turned around three times and given a stick. Each player has three chances to try to whack the piñata. Everyone takes turns until someone breaks the piñata and the goodies spill out. All the players get to share the treats!